YORK

City Theme Walks

Richard Peace

Illustrated by Paul Hannon

HILLSIDE

HILLSIDE
PUBLICATIONS
11 Nessfield Grove
Keighley
West Yorkshire
BD22 6NU

First published 1996

© Richard Peace 1996
Illustrations © Paul Hannon 1996

ISBN 1 870141 47 4

Whilst the author has walked and researched all the routes for the purposes of this guide, no responsibility can be accepted for any unforeseen circumstances encountered while following them. The publisher would, however, greatly appreciate any information regarding material changes, and also any problems encountered.

Cover illustrations
Front: York Minster
Back: St. Mary's Abbey
(Paul Hannon/Big Country Picture Library)
Page 1: 'Printer's Devil', Stonegate (Walk 3)

Printed in Great Britain by
Carnmor Print & Design
95-97 London Road
Preston
Lancashire
PR1 4BA

INTRODUCTION

York is possibly the finest city in the land to explore on foot, with history, architecture and colour at every turn. This small guide will help you enjoy its finest features. Each of the walks can easily be fitted into a leisurely day's stroll with ample time allowed for visiting the listed attractions. Their aim is to take the visitor on a fascinating time trip through York's rich historical legacy, highlighting major events without being bogged down in a wealth of incidental fact. The detailed maps are all you need to find your way around. An additional map shows the most interesting historical examples of that great British institution the pub, and the locations of attractions for children.

Each walk aims to draw together attractions within the city, linked by certain periods of history, or in the case of the last walk, an historic theme. Thus the visitor will hopefully get a feeling for that period and how York must have been during that time. The hidden worlds lurking within the modern city will be revealed. York can fairly claim to be the nation's second city in terms of historical importance, next to London: as George V noted *'the history of York is the history of England'*.

THE WALKS

1. **DIGGING DOWN TO THE PAST: ROMANS, SAXONS & VIKINGS**.............. 4
2. **ABBEYS, CHURCHES & SAINTS**.............. 9
3. **FROM NORMAN KNIGHTS TO CIVIL WAR: THE CITY WALLS**.............. 18
4. **GEORGIAN & VICTORIAN ELEGANCE**.............. 26
5. **RIVER, RAIL & TRADE**.............. 31
   APPENDIX A: CHILDREN'S ATTRACTIONS.............. 36
   APPENDIX B: HISTORIC PUBS.............. 39

USEFUL CONTACTS (York code 01904)

Tourist Information, Rougier Street: 620557   British Rail: 642155
Bus services: 624161   National Express Coaches: 0990-808080
Grand Opera House, Cumberland Street: 671818
York Film Theatre and City Screen: 612940
Joseph Rowntree Theatre: 602440
Odeon Cinema, Blossom Street: 623040
Warner Bros, Clifton Moor: 691199 (Recorded times - 691094)

① *DIGGING DOWN TO THE PAST*
ROMANS, SAXONS & VIKINGS

The Romans chose the present-day site of the Minster as their military headquarters. They first arrived in Britain in 55 B.C. and eventually came north to York (which became Roman Eboracum) in 71 A.D. after subduing local Celts hereabouts, on the edge of their empire. Although only fragments of their life here remain, it is clear they were a highly advanced and sophisticated society. Large public buildings and such features as well engineered fortifications and bathhouses attest to this. This obscure military outpost soon swelled to incorporate a civilian town and became a leading city in the Roman Empire.

Their stay lasted until the early 5th century A.D. when the classical world was falling apart and Britain was succumbing to Picts, Scots and Saxons. By the 7th century York had become capital of the Anglo-Saxon kingdom of Northumbria. By the 9th century it had been conquered by Vikings and changed its name to Jorvik.

• ***START*** *Site of the Multangular and Anglian Towers next to the library, accessed from Museum Street.*

❶ MULTANGULAR AND ANGLIAN TOWERS

The remains of Roman fortifications are found underneath later medieval construction in the small enclosed area at the back of the library, opposite the remains of St. Leonard's Hospital (see WALK 2) (access from the square in front of the library). Both sites are signed as you approach.

The red tile courses are Roman and the tower remains are one of the best preserved Roman monuments in Britain. This tower was the western corner of the walls encircling the military fortress. A strong armed presence was necessary; from 61 A.D. the famous Queen Boadicea lead Celtic tribes to slaughter tens of thousands of Romans and native collaborators. York's surrounding countryside was marsh and woodland; ideal for hostile tribes to hide in. No wonder the Romans felt the need for strong defences.

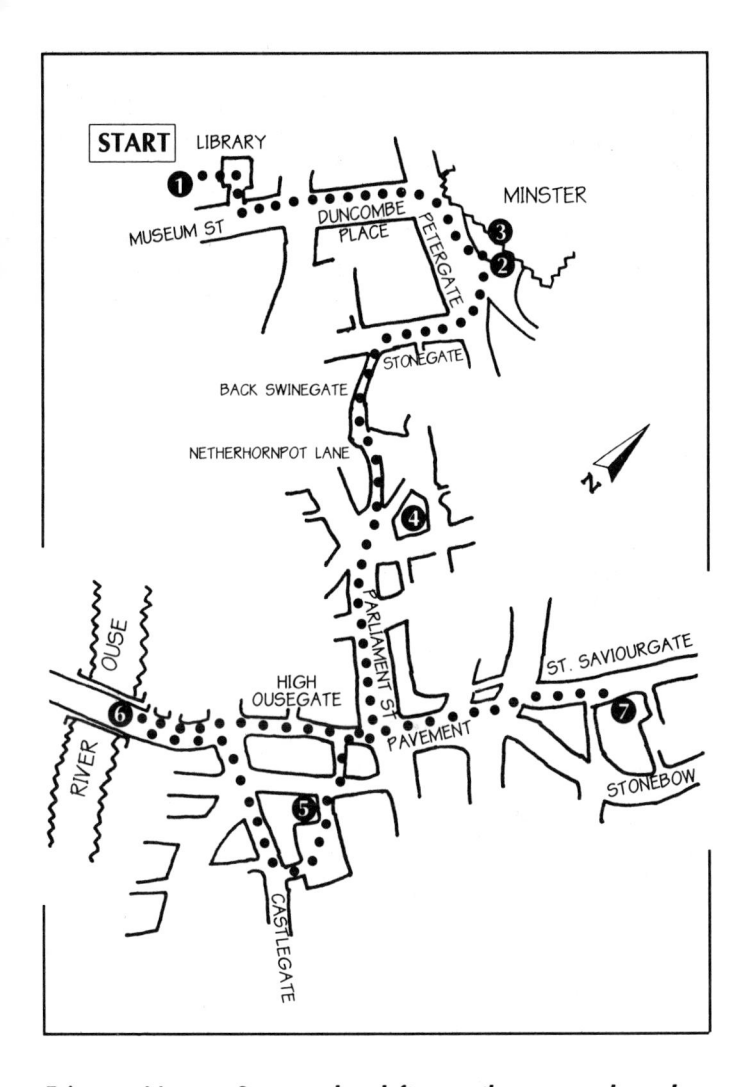

Exit onto Museum Street and go left, over the crossroads, and up Duncombe Place to the Minster. Bear right across Minster Yard to the Roman Column just before Deangate.

❷ ROMAN COLUMN

This once formed part of the Great Hall within the Roman headquarters or principia, to be visited next, in the Minster undercroft. It gives details of the legion posted within the H.Q. Its erection in 1971 marked the 1,900th anniversary of the Romans' arrival.

Enter the Minster through the doors opposite the Roman Column. The undercroft museum is on the left and downstairs as you enter. The main body of the Minster is explored in WALK 2, so try to resist the temptation to explore it now!

❸ THE UNDERCROFT

Here lie not only Roman remains but Norman features, the Minster's silver and the huge engineering works that underpin the central tower (bearing a load of 16,000 tons). The Roman basilica (public buildings used as law courts), Norman cathedral and the intact medieval building all overlap at this point. Look out for the model showing the construction of the Roman H.Q. and the eerie face remaining on the painted Roman wall.

You can also witness the spot near the exit where Constantine the Great was proclaimed Caesar in 306 A.D. and went on to become one of the greatest Roman Emperors of all time.

Exiting the Minster via the same door head across the front of St. Michael Le Belfry and left down Petergate. The first major right takes you down Stonegate. In Roman times these two roads were major transport arteries from the H.Q. finally leading out of the fortifications (Via Principalis and Via Praetoria respectively).

The first main left down Back Swinegate is marked Castle Area and Barley Hall. Bending left on this street look for the small alley, Netherhornpot Lane, on the right, emerging outside the Roman Bath public house in St. Sampson's Square.

❹ ROMAN BATH PUBLIC HOUSE

If you take a drink inside here the remains of a Roman bath are visible from the public bar through glass panels in the floor. Bathing in Roman times was a very different affair compared to today. The 'caldarium' on view in the pub was a moist heated room where dirt would be sweated out and scraped off with an edged implement. The skin's pores would then be closed with a cold plunge bath.

Out of the pub head across the square and follow down the wide shopping area of Parliament Street. At the end bend right into High Ousegate and immediate left behind All Saint's, Pavement church. Head straight on beneath the Coppergate Shopping Centre sign to arrive at the Jorvik Viking Centre on the right.

Viking warrior, Jorvik

❺ JORVIK VIKING CENTRE

Recreated here is a Coppergate alley of the 10th century, a trading area of Viking York, or Jorvik. A five and a half year dig ended in 1976 and gave the country one of its biggest ever finds of 10th century remains.

The Angles were the immediate inheritors of the Roman legacy after displacing them in the 4th century A.D., travelling from their homes in modern day Germany and Denmark. After initial plundering raids, Viking presence was officially recognised by the Anglo-Saxons in the 9th century, in the form of the

Danelaw, a huge area in the middle of England. Perhaps the strongest Viking legacy is the suffix 'gate' attached to many of the city's street names.

Open daily, April-Oct 9am-7pm Adult £4.25, Child £2.50
Nov-March 9am-5.30pm Senior citizen/student £3.15

Continue down St. Mary's Square and past the 'York Story' on the right; go right twice into Castlegate and continue to a major road junction at Nessgate. The corner of St. Michael, Spurriergate church can be seen across the busy road junction. Turn left up Lower Ousegate to bring you to the Ouse Bridge.

❻ OUSE BRIDGE

Although it may appear serene today this was the only bridge in the city in Viking times and as such connected the commercial centre of York (found outside the old Roman fortress along Ousegate, Coppergate, Pavement and Saviourgate) to national and international markets, via boats docking in this area; perhaps not as sophisticated in land based achievements as the Romans, the Vikings were supreme seamen and traders. Micklegate, on the other side of the bridge, continued the commercial area to the Roman city walls, kept standing by the Vikings.

Retrace your steps over the bridge, back in the direction you came. Follow a straight line down Ousegate and Pavement to jink left and right down St. Saviourgate. The Archaeological Resource Centre is on the right.

❼ ARCHAEOLOGICAL RESOURCE CENTRE

A visit here aims to bring alive some of the skills used by the ancient civilisations whose modern day legacy you have just witnessed. It is a fascinating insight into the archaeologist's world and techniques. Fun for all ages - the numerous 'hands-on' displays are particularly good fun for children. Houses a constantly changing variety of smaller displays.

Open Jan 2nd-mid December
Mon-Fri 10am-4pm Adult £3.50
Sat 1pm-4pm Child £2.75

② ABBEYS, CHURCHES & SAINTS

York has a long history of religion. The grand medieval gothic Minster is the most obvious sign, but a host of churches and a shrine to a Catholic saint reflect the huge variety of religious drama that York has witnessed. Forget any ideas you have of 'traditional' churches; you will experience a vast variety of architecture as well as glimpsing York's dramatic past through these buildings.

After lapsing into paganism after the Romans left, the north became officially Christian again under the Anglo-Saxon Edwin of Northumbria. The next great religious break came with the Reformation under Henry VIII, when the monarch rejected the authority of the Pope so he could remarry. He also used the opportunity to take much of the church's vast wealth for himself. Catholic resistance found expression in the Pilgrimage of Grace in which York was involved. This was a period of sad decline for the city, coinciding with economic downturn due to lost wool revenue.

A compromise was reached under Elizabeth I, which has lasted to the present day. Puritans threatened the religious order in the 17th century and tried to destroy the structure of a church based on bishoprics and devolve power to themselves. Many of the churches are still used for worship today so please respect worshippers and do not over-intrude on any service taking place.

• **START** *The grounds of St. Mary's Abbey, found in the Museum Gardens near the Yorkshire Museum.*

❶ ST. MARY'S ABBEY

These beautiful medieval ruins were once the site of the most important Benedictine monastery in the north of England. The most impressive remaining features are the window arches set against a beautiful backdrop of trees. The original abbey was built by the Normans on top of what was previously the seat of the Anglo-Saxon earls of Northumbria, a symbolic act of suppression.

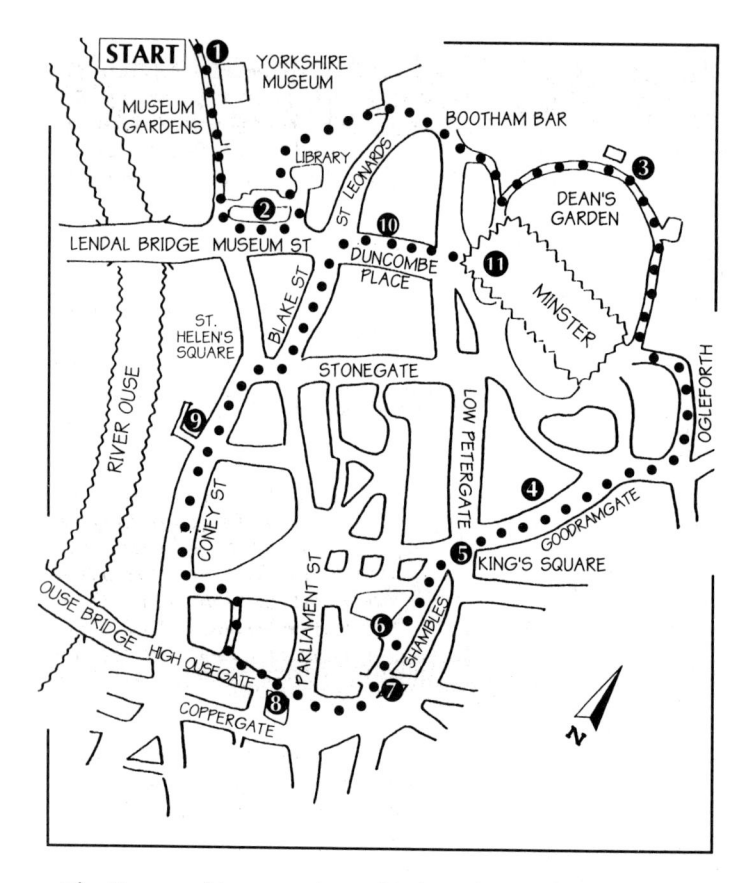

The Norman abbey grew in wealth through control of land and tax collection, so much so that in the 1260's a popular revolt forced the abbot to flee and subsequently a wall with battlements was built. The abbey closed in 1539 when Henry VIII dissolved the monasteries in order to take their wealth for himself; the royal income from confiscated lands came to one and a half million pounds, a massive sum in those days. The building was demolished over the centuries and the stone used for buildings both within York and as far away as Beverley Minster. The famous mystery plays are performed here, as the centre of the four yearly York Festival. *Free admission*

From the ruins walk across the front of the Yorkshire Museum and continue on the main path to meet the main gates on Museum Street. A small path on your left, before the gates, leads you under a vaulted passage which is a dead end, but fun to discover. Rejoin Museum Street, going left, and shortly explore the far side of St. Leonard's Hospital from the square in front of the library on your left.

❷ ST. LEONARD'S HOSPITAL

As one of the largest medieval hospitals in the north of England this is one place you definitely wouldn't want to have been around during its heyday. The main features that remain are the 13th century vaulted crypt and chapel above. As with St. Mary's the role of the building as hospital didn't survive Henry VIII's destruction of the monasteries.

The path down the right side of this open area follows the edge of the library and exits through a gate in the old city walls. Follow the path right, through large green gates and along the pedestrian way between the wall and King's Manor on the left. From Exhibition Square cross St. Leonards (the street) and through the medieval gateway of Bootham Bar. A small alleyway on the left, just before the Hole in the Wall pub, leads you away from the crowds into the fine Precentor's Court and round the corner to an incredible view of the towering heights of the Minster.

At the end of the narrow lane bear left through gates into Dean's Park. Follow the wall on the left side of this grassy space, past commemorative battle plaques, to the small building of the Minster Library on the far side.

❸ MINSTER LIBRARY

This small building is often overlooked because of its vastly grander neighbour but was itself once part of the impressive Archbishop's Palace. The Minster's original library was begun in Anglo-Saxon times but Viking raids and William the Conqueror destroyed the early collection. Today it is the largest cathedral library in the country, housing some 90,000 volumes.

Open Mon-Thur 9am-5pm, Fri 9am-12 noon
Closed weekends

Exit Dean's Park through the gates and down the cobbled Minster Yard to go first left (Chapter House Street) and bending right (Ogleforth) along these quiet backwaters. At the end of Ogleforth bear right then left by the Cross Keys pub onto the popular shopping street of Goodramgate. Shortly, on the right side of Goodramgate, a small signed gateway belies the beauty and antiquity of Holy Trinity Church.

❹ HOLY TRINITY CHURCH

Once inside this ancient church, built between 1250 and 1500, you have stepped back across the centuries. The 'viewing hole' or hagioscope, to the left of the altar, allowed the actions of two church officials to be synchronised. The most famous single item in the church is perhaps the window above the altar. You can identify the images of St. George (the English patron saint), St. John the Baptist, The Holy Trinity, St. John the Evangelist (holding a gold chalice) and St. Christopher. In the east window is St. Paulinus, who brought Christianity to York in the 7th century. Also look out for the memorial for those who met a gruesome end through the Black Death, a deadly 14th century plague that, by some estimates, killed a third of Europe at its first appearance after 1347.

It was popular for the wealthy to build chantry chapels within this church; their own special place where their soul could be prayed for. The sloping pews are some of the latest additions to the church, added around the 17th/18th century. The ramshackle lines of the church create an intimate impression of great antiquity.

Back on Goodramgate continue down the street and bear left at the first junction into King's Square. Buskers are a common sight here and it is a restful place to pause.

❺ KING'S SQUARE GRAVESTONES

A handful of old gravestones make up part of the floor on the raised area of the square. Look out for the grave of the chap who died at the age of 97 in 1761; this is the equivalent of someone living to 130 or 140 today! This is the only real proof that, until 1937, this area was a church, with animals kept ready for slaughter in the adjoining churchyard, eventually to end up in the nearby butchers' shops cramming the Shambles.

The Shambles

In the south-west corner of the square the Shambles heads off Newgate. Walking down here it is easy to see why this is one of the most famous York streets, with its ancient overhanging medieval buildings. No. 35 on the right hand side is now a shrine to Margaret Clitherow.

❻ THE SHAMBLES

About halfway down on the right note the incongruous house marked as a shrine to Margaret of Clitherow. She was unlucky enough to be a principled woman in the midst of religious upheaval, when little more than a century before her time her Catholic religion had been unquestionably the national faith. Protestant doctrine had infiltrated England at many levels, and a compromise was finally reached under Elizabeth I, though even such an agreement had its victims such as Margaret of Clitherow.

Elizabeth attacked both Catholics and Puritans, who both wanted to pull the national religion in radically different directions. For harbouring Jesuits (extreme Catholic priests), Margaret was 'pressed' to death by having heavy stones laid on her.

England during this period must have been a frightening and disturbing place, with extreme views on both sides intensified in the 1580's as Jesuits from Europe, the 'secret agents' of Catholicism, began to infiltrate England. In the last 30 years of Elizabeth's reign around 300 Catholics were executed for treason.

Immediately at the end of the Shambles cross the small courtyard on the left towards St. Crux church.

❼ ST. CRUX

Now used as a parish room the interior is strikingly bright and pretty. Used for jumble sales and coffee mornings it is usually possible to get a coffee inside and relax whilst admiring the interior. There are some fine restored monuments inside including the colourful monument to Robert Watter and many memorials to a variety of professions and trades from the city in centuries past. Many of the monuments were salvaged from a much more ancient church, demolished in the 19th century.

Continuing away from the Shambles head right up Pavement, another main shopping area. At the first junction continue on towards the distinctive spire of All Saints, Pavement ahead of you, going up High Ousegate to the entrance.

❽ ALL SAINTS, PAVEMENT

The distinctive lantern tower gives this church much of its fame and interest; the structure you see today is a replica of the medieval original, which was lit at night to guide travellers coming through the nearby forests and marshes to York. Some of the lenses used in the tower are inside the church. Be careful when you enter via the north door; the knocker on it is a depiction of the mouth of hell! The Great East and West Windows contain depictions of saints and scenes from the Passion and are works of art in their own right. Also look out for the shields of medieval guilds on the south wall.

Resuming up the shopping precinct of High Ousegate look for a very narrow footway on the right (just before what is currently Dillon's Bookshop). The high brick walls of this well used thoroughfare widen to join another precinct, Market Street. Heading left into Market Street emerge into yet another wide busy shopping area, Coney Street, and go right. Towards the end of the street on the left see:

York Minster

❾ ST. MARTIN-LE-GRAND

Part traditional church and part garden! The original 15th century church was gutted by fire during a 1942 air raid, which meant its restoration was adapted because of extensive damage. The 'interior' consists of the old tower and south aisle, whilst the remainder of the building has been converted into a garden of remembrance for the dead of the two world wars. Another unusual feature is the 17th century clock which overhangs Coney Street. The Great West Window inside is considered one of the best 15th century windows in the country.

At the end of Coney Street, emerging into St. Helen's Square, you can visit the church of the same name on the opposite side of the square, itself originally a churchyard. From outside the church head up Blake Street on the left, and at its end bear diagonally right across Duncombe Place to the obvious and imposing French Gothic tower and facade of St. Wilfrid's.

❿ ST. WILFRID

Perhaps the most sumptuous interior of any church in York. The high vaulted roof, rich decorations and clear continental influence reflect yet another element in York's rich religious tapestry. Colourful and intricate the church still retains an awe-inspiring capacity. It bears the name of a former 7th and 8th century Bishop of York, who was also a great pioneer of the new Roman church against the Celtic, and built many monasteries and churches.

The obvious climax comes with a visit to the Minster. Simply head up Duncombe Place and through the main doors.

⓫ YORK MINSTER

The largest Gothic church in northern Europe, built over a 250 year timespan! With no less than 128 windows, the Minster is superb from any viewpoint. It merits a book in itself but a brief summary of its main features accompanies the plan opposite. This contains just a few of literally hundreds of interesting features: the Minster Bookshop can supply much greater detail.

YORK MINSTER - a brief guide

- **LADY CHAPEL**
Contains Great East Window, the size of a tennis court, and the largest single area of medieval glass in the world.

- **CHOIR**
The crypt is accessed from the south choir aisle. Includes the Norman Doomstone depicting Hell and the seven deadly sins, and 12th century tomb of William of York whose shrine was destroyed during the Reformation as miracles were said to occur here.

Standing by the choir screen it is possible to look up 200ft (60m) into the central tower.

- **SOUTH TRANSEPT**
Dating from 13th century. Contains Rose Window with red and white roses commemorating end of Wars of the Roses, 1486. Severely damaged in 1984 fire and restored in 1987.

Contains tomb of Archbishop de Grey, 13th century. Objects found within it are now in Undercroft. Staff plunged into dragon at his feet symbolises conquest of evil

- **CHAPTER HOUSE**
Contains impressive domed roof, with no supporting pillars to take the weight.

- **NORTH TRANSEPT**
Contains Five Sisters window dating from 1260. The 100,000 pieces of glass were taken out for safety during World War Two and later re-assembled.

The huge astronomical clock on the east side commemorates the loss of 18,000 airmen in that same war, stationed in the north-east of England.

- shop

- **NAVE**
Contains Great West Window and twin west towers. The SW tower houses 'Great Peter', a 20 ton bell.

- Great West Door, exterior surrounded by 9-inch (22cm) figures telling the story of Adam & Eve.

③ *NORMAN KNIGHTS TO CIVIL WAR*
A WALK ROUND THE CITY WALLS

Next to the Minster, the walls are one of York's most famous features. They reflect the feeling of many medieval rulers that York, as the capital of the North, had to be well secured against rivals who claimed to be legitimate leaders of the country. York was at the centre of two bloody conflicts which sprang from this disputed legitimacy; the Wars of the Roses and the Civil War. The former was born from the dispute between the aristocratic houses of Lancaster and York as to which line was the true successor to the throne, the latter from a challenge by the forces of Parliament to the legitimacy of the throne itself. For periods of medieval history York was more important than London; it was during this time that the Dukedom of York was first conferred on the monarch's second son (as it still is today).
NB: THE WALLS ARE CLOSED BETWEEN DUSK AND DAWN

- **START** Southern side of Lendal Bridge.

Heading away from the southern side of Lendal Bridge turn right onto the walls and climb over the arch over the road, following the walls to get a good view over the railway area. The wall turns left at Tofts tower to come to Micklegate Bar.

❶ MICKLEGATE BAR

Undoubtedly the most important gate into the city; most sovereigns in the country's history have entered the city through this gateway. The front of the bar carries both the arms of the city of York and those of Edward III. The site is gruesomely famous as the place where so-called traitors had their heads displayed on poles; Richard of York (Wars of the Roses, 1460) and Jacobite traitors (1746) were amongst the unfortunate. The bar houses Micklegate Bar Museum which tells the historic story of the walls.

Open 9am to dusk
Adult £1.50, Concession £1, Child 50p

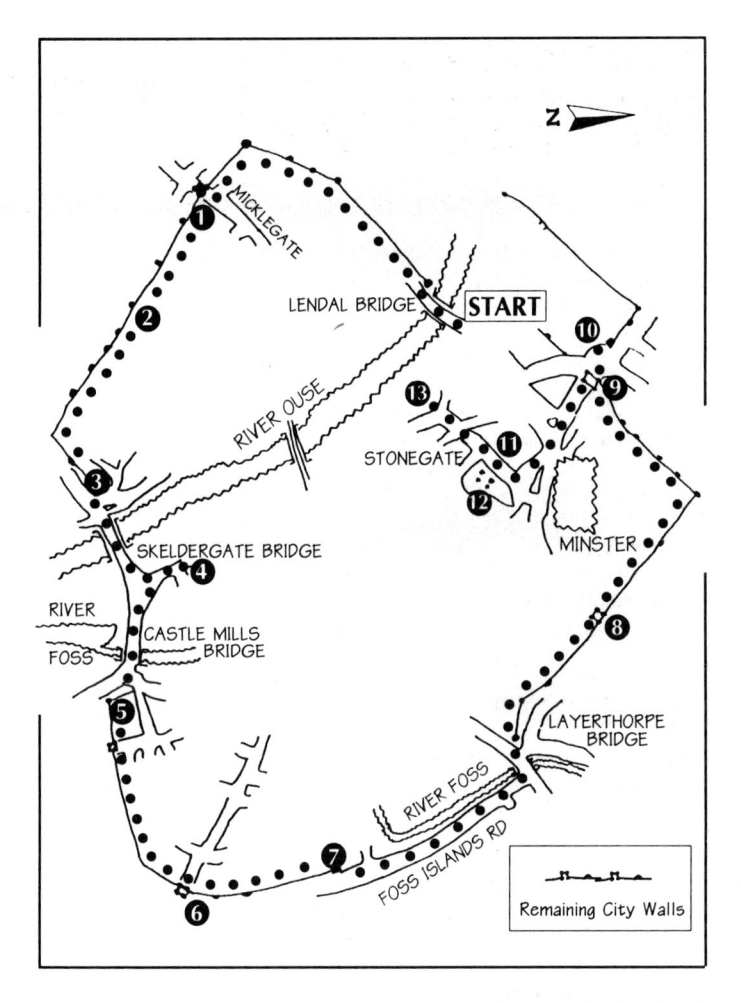

Resuming on the walls pass over Victoria Bar, above the back to back Victorian terraces of this southern area of the city (see WALK 4). The wall bends left passing over the Bitchdaughter or Sadler Tower. From here you get a good idea of the amount of work and sophisticated level of construction that has gone into the walls, as they stretch away in either direction.

❷ THE CITY WALLS

This walk takes in the remaining sections of the medieval walls, dating from the 13th and 14th centuries, along with their fortified gates or 'bars'. The majority of the medieval walls still remain; occasional sections have been demolished to make way for more recent developments such as St. Leonard's Place.

A great debt is owed to local cityfolk whose vehement protest in the 19th century prevented the complete demolition of the walls by the city authorities! Without them you would not be able to get such unique views over the city, nor appreciate how far the city has spread outside its medieval confines, marked by the wall boundary.

Carry on the next short stretch of wall descending to Skeldergate Bridge, past the grassy tree-covered mound of Baile Hill on the left.

❸ BAILE HILL

This mound is the site of the later of two castles built by William the Conqueror to suppress the local Saxon rising. He had arrived in England in 1066 with a very dubious claim to the throne, based on a pact made with a distant relative of the Saxon King of England. He made good this claim by military force but needed to consolidate his new kingdom in the north. The earlier fortification opposite this site is now Clifford's Tower.

From Baile Hill head over Skeldergate Bridge and left at the roundabout. Clifford's Tower is just a little way down on the right.

❹ CLIFFORD'S TOWER

Originally a Norman fortress of wood, its defences were completed by damming the Foss and creating the 'King's Fishpond' which also acted as a food supply. It takes its name from Roger Clifford, who was hung from the tower wrapped in chains in the 14th century. The tower was later fortified in stone and used at one time as the royal mint (for royal coin production). It later fell into disuse and was even utilised as an ornamental folly as part of larger gardens. There are magnificent views from the walk around the edge of its upper storey.

Open   Easter-Sept 10am-6pm;   Oct-Easter 10am-4pm
Adult   £1.60, Concession   £1.20, Child 80p

*The City Walls
near Lendal Bridge,
looking to the Minster*

Retrace your steps to the roundabout and go over Castle Mills Bridge. The distinctive shape of Fishergate Postern Tower ahead allows you access onto the eastern section of wall.

❺ FISHERGATE POSTERN TOWER & FISHERGATE BAR

The arched gateway in the side was known as the Postern. Note the projecting first floor lavatory which once discharged straight into the King's Pool below. Having mounted the walls drop to pass Fishergate Bar. Although one of six lesser gateways to the city it still saw violent action in 1489, when the peasants hereabouts rioted and set fire to the gateway as a protest against heavy taxation (inviting comparisons with the 'Poll Tax' riots during Mrs. Thatcher's time as Prime Minister). Look for the scorch marks beneath the central arch.

Follow this section, with more modern development either side of the walls, and come to:

21

⑥ WALMGATE BAR

Unique amongst the 'bars' of York as it retains its barbican, or frontal defences. An elegant white construction on the rear adds to the gate's distinction. This area took the brunt of the city seige during the Civil War. The forces of Parliament were fighting what they saw as arbitrary royal power, which manifested itself in such acts as illegal tax gathering.

In 1644 the Parliamentarians besieged York and were beaten back to nearby Marston Moor. However they won the battle and renewed a successful siege. Thankfully York was spared complete wanton destruction. Look for bullet marks on the front of the barbican as signs of the siege. The arms of Henry V remain on the front of the bar.

The remaining short section of wall emerges on Foss Islands Road by:

⑦ THE RED TOWER

Dating from 1490 this building marked the edge of the King's Pool lake. It was extensively damaged and later used as stables and for gunpowder manufacture. No wall was ever built between here and Layerthorpe Bridge as the area originally contained a natural barrier of treacherous marshland.

Walk up Foss Islands Road, past a small green bridge on your left, to bring you to a roadbridge (Layerthorpe Bridge). Bear left over the bridge and rejoin the walls on the other side of the road. The River Foss marks the boundary of the King's Pool prior to rejoining the walls. By the late 18th century it had silted up; the river was channelled and Foss Islands Road later constructed. Back on the city walls you eventually reach Monk Bar.

⑧ MONK BAR

The tallest, most easily defended bar of the walls. Really it is a self contained fortress, each floor defensible even if the others have been taken. On the exterior is the Plantagenet coat of arms (a royal dynasty including 8 kings of England). Now it houses the Richard III museum. This Yorkist monarch was vilified in history as the murderer of two young princes. The display inside the museum here aims to redress the balance.

Richard III himself, who spent much time in the north, built up his political power base here. He was very popular with York citizens of the time. The section from Monk Bar to Bootham Bar is the most heavily defended part of the walls, reflecting the fact it was from the north, and against this section of wall, that Scots attacked in medieval times. Note the unusual figures on top of the tower, ready to hurl boulders on attackers.

Admission £1   Concessions 50p

Monk Bar

The section from Monk Bar to Bootham Bar gives you arguably the finest of wall views, taking you behind the Treasurer's House, Minster Library and several splendid residences. Lots of great photo opportunities! Eventually emerge to finish the wall section at:

⑨ BOOTHAM BAR

Standing on the site of a Roman gate this is the oldest bar of the walls. It retains its portcullis in fixed position, thankfully saved in the 19th century by local conservationists. Guards stood here in medieval times to welcome in travellers from the nearby Forest of Galtres and to protect them from wolves. In its original form the bar was joined to the wall of the huge St. Mary's Abbey.

Head away from the city walls towards the facade of the Art Gallery, across Exhibition Square. In the square, in front of the gallery, look for an entrance on the left leading to:

⑩ THE KING'S MANOR

Originally part of St. Mary's Abbey it became the home of the King's Council in the North, shortly after the dissolution of the monasteries. James I and Charles I both stayed here.
Admission free. Public canteen.

Clifford's Tower

Retrace your steps under Bootham Bar and follow Petergate past the Minster and St. Michael Le Belfrey on the left, turning onto Stonegate on the right. Shortly on your right a sign for the Stonegate Gallery leads you to:

⑪ REMAINS OF TWELFTH CENTURY HOUSE

Undoubtedly the oldest dwelling house remnants of any substance in York. Remains of two sides of the building are attached to adjoining buildings; the windows would have had shutters rather than glass and the building may have had an undercroft.

Further down Stonegate on the left Coffee Yard (look for the red devil at its entrance) leads to:

⓬ BARLEY HALL

With its houses packed together, this alley gives a feel for medieval York. The Barley Hall project of York Archaeological Trust has restored a former Priory hospice and house to give a taste of medieval life in the city.

Return to Stonegate and continue on into St. Helen's Square. Facing you is the cream and mauve facade of the Mansion House (described and illustrated in WALK 4). Just to the right of this building a passage takes you down to the main doors of:

⓭ THE GUILDHALL

A guildhall has stood on this site since the 14th century. A German bomb wiped out hundreds of years of history when it landed on the hall in 1942. Originally the 'entertainment complex' of York it was used for pageants and festivities and today houses a go-ahead city council. It is difficult to tell this is not the genuine medieval building, but a 20th century reconstruction. Only more modern features like the beautiful stained glass show some concession to changing fashion.

Micklegate Bar

④ GEORGIAN & VICTORIAN ELEGANCE

Whilst York is perhaps most famed for its medieval buildings (and remains of even earlier civilisations) it contains a wealth of architecture and history from Georgian and Victorian times. After the Civil War trade and manufacture declined, but much 18th century architecture reflects the fact York was then a social capital for the local gentry from surrounding areas. Indeed York became a very popular place in which to have a town house, which provided a welcome break from country life. Coffee houses and the racecourse became highly fashionable meeting places.

Although this walk doesn't feature major 'stars' such as the Minster it will take you off the tourist trail to see how the town developed in the eras after the great Civil War, when people's minds turned away from military struggle and self-preservation to classical refinement in the arts, such influence penetrating down to the more humble buildings you encounter.

The delicate and elegant Georgian style is as much a part of York's beauty as the large 'crowd-pullers'. The old historic core to the south of the Minster was retained, land to the south-west and near the confluence of the Ouse and Foss being chosen for building during this period. If you have exhausted the possibilities of the main sights why not add a further dimension to your visit.

- **START** Dick Turpin's Grave, St. George's Churchyard

❶ DICK TURPIN'S GRAVE

The incongruous newer housing estates add a surreal note to a visit to the grave of one of England's most famous and over-romanticised criminals. This mid-18th century highwayman, smuggler and thief has been the stereotypical model for countless books and films on such themes. Turpin had fled north from his Essex homelands to avoid capture. When the authorities eventually caught up with him he was brought to York in 1739 and hanged. Although stolen, his body was later reburied. John Palmer was the 'everyday' name he took when he resettled and reinvented himself in East Yorkshire.

From the graveyard turn right out of the exit and bend right round the corner towards Fishergate Postern Tower, with its distinctive tiled roof, then left onto Piccadilly and right over Castle Mills Bridge. Staying on the right over the bridge the back of the assize courts greet you on the right. Go round to the front, to the 'eye', but note that the other attractions here such as Clifford's Tower and the Castle Museum are covered elsewhere.

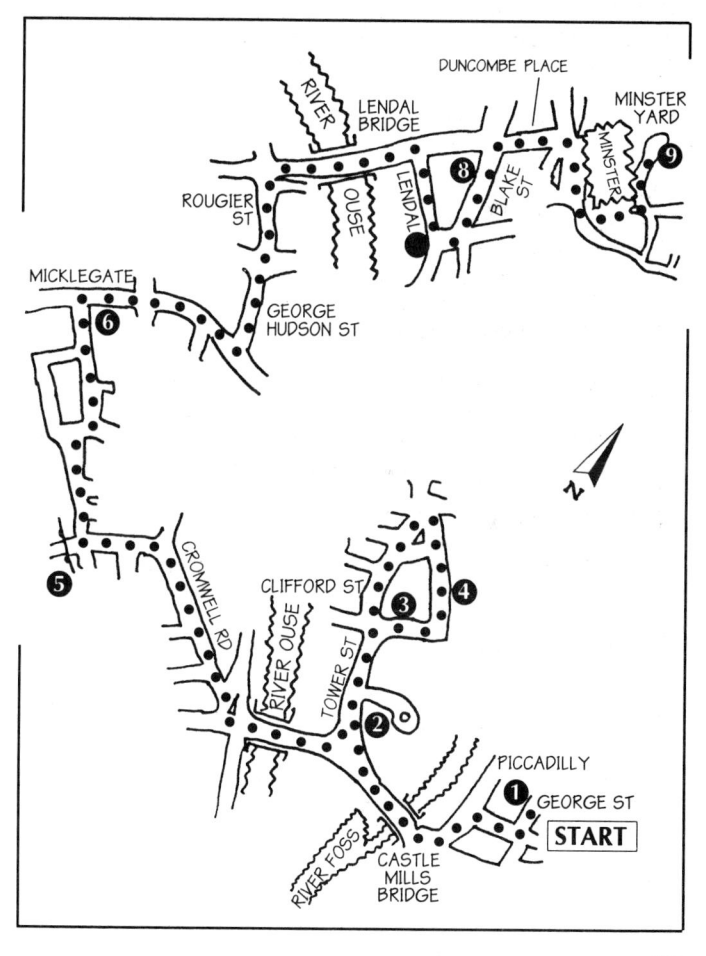

❷ ASSIZE COURTS

A beautiful symmetrical facade shows how the influence of ancient Greece surfaced in Georgian times. The columns and portico facing the eye reflect ancient, classical designs. More recently the courts witnessed such dramatic trials as those of Dick Turpin and Luddites (early 19th century rioters against the introduction of basic machinery). Now used as the local crown courts, with public gallery.

Continue up Tower Street to the first crossroads reached. Find the Regimental Museum as Tower Street bends right, opposite a car park.

❸ REGIMENTAL MUSEUM

Based on the history of two regiments that recruit in Yorkshire this museum also shows the visitor how vast areas of the Empire were won, and some lost, largely during Georgian and Victorian times. Models of major battles bring the process to life but it is the wealth of costumes and medal displays, with accompanying personal testimonies that are perhaps most poignant.

Open Mon-Sat 9am-4.30pm   Adult £1 Child/pensioner 50p

Retrace steps and go right onto Clifford Street which offers the fine ornate brick magistrates' courts, the Yorks Institute (now York Dungeon) and the Opera House. Just past the latter, loop back 180 degrees right and head down Castlegate to Fairfax House on the left.

❹ FAIRFAX HOUSE

One of the finest townhouses in England, this masterpiece was, prior to the 1980's, part of a cinema, then dance hall. It houses a superb 18th century furniture collection. Fantastic plaster ceilings and sumptuous period decor create a beautifully delicate atmosphere.

Open 19th Feb-6th Jan Mon-Sat 11am-5pm   Adult £3
Sun 1.30pm-5pm Closed Fridays

Head back south-east onto Tower Street to cross the Skeldergate Bridge on the right over the Ouse. Just over the bridge head sharp right into Skeldergate and immediately split off left up Cromwell Road, just inside Baile Hill. Head through this quiet residential district until meeting the Golden Ball pub (parts of a typical Victorian interior still retained) and head left down Victor Street towards:

❺ VICTORIA BAR

This entrance through the city walls was constructed in 1837, the year Queen Victoria came to the throne. It provided access between Bishophill, inside the city walls, and Nunnery Lane outside. The houses round and about are typical Victorian 'back to backs'.

Just before the bar Lower Priory Street, on the right, leads to St. Columbus and straight across the junction to Priory Street. Half way along the latter the dominating brick structure is the:

❻ ASSEMBLY OF GOD CHURCH

The Wesleyans who originally built this church in the 1850's were non-conformists. Rejecting Catholicism and the compromise state religion, they wanted to control the administration of religion themselves. This spacious building is the second largest auditorium in the city after the Minster. Art nouveau glasswork complements the renovated interior. It is now used by the 'new wave' religion of its title and preachers have included Billy Graham.

The Mansion House

Turn right into Micklegate with a fine parade of Georgian residences and the outstanding Falcon Inn. Also look for Micklegate House on the left with its commemorative plaque. Continue down Micklegate and left down George Hudson Street, past Porter's Bar, to Station Road and right to cross Lendal Bridge. First right over it takes you onto Lendal at the end of which you find yourself in St. Helen's Square with, on the right, the mauve and cream facade of the:

❼ MANSION HOUSE

Beautiful mid-18th century symmetrical architecture provides the official residence of York's Lord Mayor whilst in office. Although not normally open to the public there are occasional open days with a small entry fee for charity, or you may make a special visit by prior application at the discretion of the Lord Mayor.

On the left side of St. Helen's Square exit on Blake Street to find, on the left, the imposing stone portico of the:

❽ ASSEMBLY ROOMS

Restored to their former glory in 1951 these sumptuous buildings reflect one of the great social trends of the mid-18th century; elegant dances. Originally an orchestra would play for the landed gentry who came from round and about to 'strut their stuff'. The orchestra would walk under the floor which was specially constructed with springs, to make it suitable for dancing. The rooms now offer fine quality tea, coffee and meals, or you may just wander around.

Continue to the end of Blake Street and right up Duncombe Place. Go round the south side of the Minster until opposite St. William's and head left up Minster Yard to the National Trust's Treasurer's House.

❾ TREASURER'S HOUSE

The title bears witness to the fact this was originally the site of the house of the keeper of the Minster's affairs. However the current 18th century construction was restored by an industrialist in the early 20th century, the religious role of the building having vanished after the reformation. James I, Charles I, James II and Elizabeth II have all been entertained here during visits to York.

Open 1st April-31st October   Adult £3 Child £1.50
10.30am-5pm

⑤ RIVER, RAIL & TRADE

River transport was vital to York's trade as early as Viking times; the Ouse linked them to the North Sea via the Humber estuary. The Foss was more important in providing part of the medieval defences. It was once dammed to create a large pond used for fishing and to feed the moats that surrounded the two Norman castles. Railway came much later, in the mid-19th century, but provided a magnificent architectural legacy for the city to complement its more ancient areas. In the 20th century it also became a mainstay of the local economy.

This walk will get you right away from the tourist crowds to some of York's more tranquil spots. It is such a pleasure to see that, unlike the case in so many British cities, York has not become the servant of the car but still values its rail and water links; ways of travelling that have their own civilised charm, which you can experience here.

- **START** York Railway Station

❶ YORK RAILWAY STATION & STATION HOTEL

Perhaps not an immediately obvious choice but the graceful curves of the triple arched roof are quite a sight; there is still something of the drama that would have been created by this setting in Victorian times, though the steam trains have been replaced by less romantic modern engines. When built it was thought to be one of the greatest stations of the world. The newly named Royal York Hotel shows the kind of opulence that would have greeted the 'better' class of visitor arriving here.

Head left out of the station (with an optional visit to Rail Rider's World on your left) and follow Station Road to the first left, and left again up Leeman Road. Under the railway bridge you'll find the main entrance to the National Railway Museum.

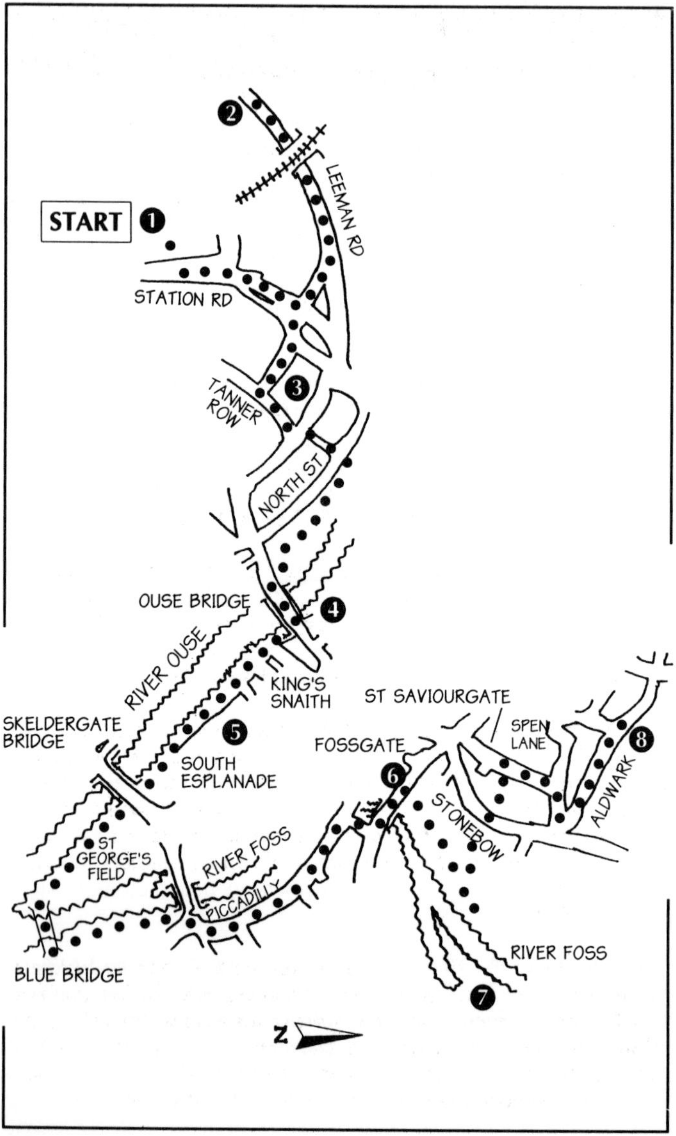
START
LEEMAN RD
STATION RD
TANNER ROW
NORTH ST
OUSE BRIDGE
RIVER OUSE
KING'S SNAITH
ST SAVIOURGATE
SPEN LANE
SKELDERGATE BRIDGE
FOSSGATE
SOUTH ESPLANADE
ALDWARK
STONEBOW
ST GEORGE'S FIELD
RIVER FOSS
PICCADILLY
RIVER FOSS
BLUE BRIDGE
N

❷ NATIONAL RAILWAY MUSEUM

The trains themselves are the stars of this nationally famous museum. Housed in the old Leeman Road steam depot, and a newly constructed larger building, this museum quickly became the most popular in the north of England after its opening in 1975. The royal carriages used by such monarchs as Victoria and Edward VII on visits around the country are of almost unbelievable opulence. Later classics include the Mallard, holder of the world steam train speed record (126mph in 1938). Also contains a cafe.

Open Mon-Sat 10am-6pm   Adult £4.50 Child £2.50
Sun 11am-6pm   Family/concession tickets

Retrace your steps to the junction with Station Road. Head straight across under the arch of the city walls by the statue of George Leeman and to the War Memorial on the right. Continuing straight on you find yourself in front of:

❸ BRITISH RAIL HEADQUARTERS BUILDING

This building's opulent style reflects the wealth made from the growth of the railways. Finished in 1906 it still houses the central administration for British Rail Eastern Region. Reflecting many architectural styles it might look more at home on the continent. It stands opposite what was the original Station Hotel.

Through the black iron gates past the building turn left onto Tanner Row and continue straight across George Hudson Street down a narrow lane by the Corner Pin pub. Cross over the road to the terrace garden, with good views of Lendal Bridge, the Guildhall and the disused Yorkshire Herald Building. Bear right and follow the riverside path in front of the Moat Hotel. Steps bring you to:

❹ OUSE BRIDGE

In Viking times this was the only bridge over the whole of the Ouse. It also carried the main road from London to the north. The medieval bridge here housed numerous buildings. The river was tidal until the 18th century when boats navigated as far as here from the North Sea. In 1829 the much hated toll system over the bridge was abolished. Today it is simply one of many crossings over the river.

Turn left and cross over Ouse Bridge, and on the far side take steps down to the river on the right. Past the King's Arms you are now on King's Staith, with the Ouse on the right. The South Esplanade then leads you to Skeldergate Bridge.

❺ OUSE BRIDGE TO SKELDERGATE BRIDGE

This stretch of the waterfront may be crowded in summer but outside high tourist season it is usually pleasantly quiet. There are good views of the cargo loading facilities on the opposite bank of Queen's Staith, which handled butter, coal and cocoa beans in the 17th century. Centuries before this, both Romans and Vikings had used the river to invade this hostile northern area. Thankfully, today the river is used mostly by travellers or for recreation.

Past the old Friary wall stay on the path under Skeldergate Bridge through the small park area of St. George's Field, until you see the River Foss join from the left at Blue Bridge. Over Blue Bridge head left by the large open area and strange tower over the Foss - a modern day flood defence system. Passing Castle Mills Lock emerge on the eastern side of Castle Mills Bridge. Cross the ring road to head up Piccadilly by Fishergate Postern Tower. After going right in front of the Red Lion pub a sign immediately directs you left up Fossgate to the Merchant Adventurers' Hall.

Merchant Adventurers' Hall

⑥ MERCHANT ADVENTURERS' HALL

Just over Fossgate Bridge an ornate brick archway guides you to this huge timber framed hall. It derives its name from a powerful medieval trading organisation which handled foreign and York based trade. Be sure to look at the undercroft and chapel as well.

After admiring some of the superb facades on Fossgate head down the narrow Straker's Passage, almost opposite Merchant Adventurers' Hall. Head right in front of the modern British Telecom building and straight on to a sitting area in front of the river. To the right is the bridge over the Foss and to the left is:

⑦ ROWNTREE WAREHOUSE

Once a flour mill, this large turreted building was taken over by the locally famous chocolate company to handle cocoa beans. It was supposed to become a visitor attraction with a planned 'Rowntree Chocolate Experience' but it proved too expensive in times of recession. Now the only boat of any size on this quiet river is the vessel bringing newsprint to the Yorkshire Evening Press nearby.

Complete this small loop by the river by heading left in front of the large car park and back towards the Telecom building, and straight on up the signed Black Horse Passage to Stonebow. Another small passage opposite Garden Place (High Hungate) leads to the left of a church (now an Archaeology centre). Head right down the elegant St. Saviourgate and right onto Spen Lane at the end. Bend sharp left onto Aldwark. At the end of this quiet residential street, set back in its own grounds is:

⑧ MERCHANT TAYLORS' HALL

In the 17th century some trading companies required a royal charter (i.e. permission) to operate. Merchant Taylors was one such example. A craft guild incorporating tailors, drapers and hosiers had its base in the 14th century Great Hall of this building. The Great Hall still has its original roof whilst the Little Hall has heraldic glass windows. Used as a theatre in the 17th and 18th centuries, it still retains a minstrels' gallery.

Open April-Oct   Mondays only. Admission Free.

Ⓐ CHILDREN'S ATTRACTIONS

The following are not exclusively for children but the content or presentation of the attractions will have special appeal to the younger generation.

• *For younger children..........................*

❶ MUSEUM OF AUTOMATA
An incredible collection of 'automata' or mechanised models which aim to copy natural movement. Includes separate collections of miniatures, French pieces and robots amongst many other attractions. Also includes pieces that may be operated by children themselves.
Open daily 9.30am-5.30pm (January 10am-4pm)

❷ FRIARGATE MUSEUM
Model wax figures of important characters in history, politics and many other spheres.
Open from 10am (closed Fridays)

❸ YORK MODEL RAILWAY
A third of a mile of miniature track contains fascinating detail, including 2500 people, 600 buildings, 1000 vehicles, 5000 trees and 2000 lights, all recreated in painstaking detail.
Open daily (except Christmas and Boxing Day)
March-Oct 9.30am-6pm; Nov-Feb 10.30am-5pm

❹ JORVIK VIKING CENTRE
Powered cars take you back through the world of Viking villagers. Life-like figures, smells and all types of construction submerge you in the past.
Open daily (except Christmas Day)
1st Nov-31st March 9am-5.30pm
1st April-31st Oct 9am-7pm

❺ YORKSHIRE MUSEUM OF FARMING
Set in 8 acres of parkland at Murton, 3 miles from York. Tools, implements and tractors are complemented by a chance for younger children to pet pigs, calves and sheep. Ideal for those long sunny days.
Open March-end Oct. For hours phone 01904-489966

• *For older children...............*

❻ YORK CASTLE MUSEUM
Ideal for older children is England's most popular museum of everyday life. Based on a York doctor's collection of everyday objects, it has since been vastly enlarged from these humble origins. Contains great visual appeal, with such features as completely reconstructed 'typical' household rooms spanning Jacobean, Georgian and Victorian times up to the 1950's. There is a completely reconstructed Edwardian Street and the cell were Dick Turpin was held can be seen. There are a host of other great attractions including a working mill.
Open April-Oct 9.30am (Sun 10am)-5.30pm
Nov-March 9.30am (Sun 10am)-4pm

❼ THE YORKSHIRE MUSEUM
The finest collections of archaeology, geology, and natural history in the north of England. There are new galleries with the emphasis on everyday life in Roman, Anglo-Saxon and Viking times. Built on the original site of St. Mary's Abbey it tells its story.
Open daily April-Oct 10am-5pm
Nov-March 10am-5pm (Sunday 1pm-5pm)

❽ THE YORK STORY
A highly inventive exploration of 1000 years of York's history. The highlight is an incredible reconstruction of the dangers of medieval cathedral building.
Open 10am-5pm (Sun 1pm-5pm)

❾ ARC ARCHAEQLOGICAL CENTRE
A 'hands-on' experience where the children work with real archaeologists. Videos, lectures and practical exercises.
Open 10am-4pm (Sat 1pm-4pm)

❿ THE YORK DUNGEON
A real chamber of horrors! Not for the unaccompanied child or those of a nervous disposition. Historically based displays focusing on such figures as Margaret Clitherow, Guy Fawkes and Dick Turpin but with plenty of dramatic ghoulish gore!
Open 10am-5.30pm (10am-4.30pm Oct-March)

• NB: York City Council produces a leaflet showing establishments with facilities for the very young.

YORK

● CHILDREN'S ATTRACTIONS
■ PRESERVED HISTORIC PUBS

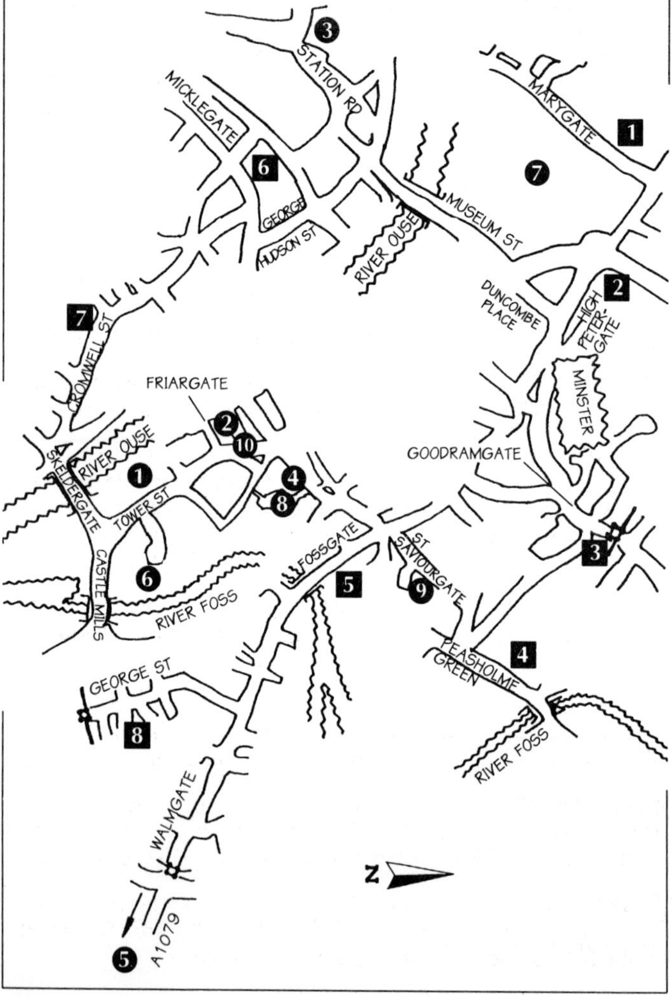

Ⓑ PRESERVED HISTORIC PUBS

The following are listed for the quality and authenticity of their interiors. Because interiors have generally been poorly protected by the law they have been much altered, especially by many brewery companies that own the pubs. Those mentioned, to varying degrees, preserve something of the original layout, or at least pre-second world war 'refits'. Thus this list concentrates on originality rather than modern and largely false attempts to recreate a feeling of antiquity for tourists.

1 MINSTER INN 24 Marygate. This is a small Edwardian pub with a very traditional layout of four areas; public bar, private back room, smoke room and back lounge. Many parts are still as they were when the pub was designed and built in 1903.

2 YORK ARMS 26 High Petergate. This Victorian pub dating from 1838 was saved from 'remodelling' in 1978. Instead of destroying the historic core of the old pub a new lounge was built onto the side.

3 ROYAL OAK 18 Goodramgate. Well preserved inter-war layouts are extremely rare but these three separate rooms are a fine example.

4 BLACK SWAN 23 Peasholme Green. A blend of styles from throughout the ages; 17th century fireplaces, doorways, a staircase and oak panelling blend with a 1930's restructuring to give a unique atmosphere. Reputedly the birthplace of General Wolfe, a famous soldier in the 18th century campaign against the French in Canada.

5 BLUE BELL 53 Fossgate. Perfectly preserved Edwardian refurbishment. Authentic panels and glass screens make this pub unique in York. Indeed, such preservation is extremely rare in the whole UK.

6 THE FALCON 94 Micklegate. Originally a coaching inn, in Victorian times the premises were converted to provide for the then new fashion of 'stand up' drinking at a service counter.

7 THE GOLDEN BALL 2 Cromwell Road. Although a pub for locals away from the tourist heart of York, it retains much Victorian charm. The back lounge is original, other areas are from a 1920's remodelling.

8 THE PHOENIX 75 George Street. Dating from the 1830's, the oldest existing parts, from the end of the 19th century, are to be found near the front of the building, including a fine screen.

HILLSIDE GUIDES - ACROSS THE NORTH

Long Distance Walks
- **THE COAST TO COAST WALK**
- **FURNESS WAY**
- **DALES WAY COMPANION**
- **CLEVELAND WAY COMPANION**
- **THE WESTMORLAND WAY**
- **THE CUMBERLAND WAY**
- **NORTH BOWLAND TRAVERSE**
- **LADY ANNE'S WAY**

Circular Walks - Lancashire
- **BOWLAND**
- **PENDLE & THE RIBBLE**

Circular Walks - Yorkshire Dales
- **HOWGILL FELLS**
- **THREE PEAKS**
- **MALHAMDALE**
- **WHARFEDALE**
- **NIDDERDALE**
- **WENSLEYDALE**
- **SWALEDALE**

Circular Walks - North York Moors
- **WESTERN MOORS**
- **SOUTHERN MOORS**
- **NORTHERN MOORS**

Circular Walks - South Pennines
- **BRONTE COUNTRY**
- **CALDERDALE**
- **ILKLEY MOOR**

Circular Walks - Peak District
- **NORTHERN PEAK**
- **CENTRAL PEAK**

Circular Walks - North Pennines
- **TEESDALE**
- **EDEN VALLEY**

Hillwalking - Lake District
- **OVER LAKELAND MOUNTAINS**
- **OVER LAKELAND FELLS**

Yorkshire Pub Walks
- **HARROGATE/WHARFE VALLEY**
- **HAWORTH/AIRE VALLEY**

Large format colour hardback
FREEDOM OF THE DALES

BIKING COUNTRY
- **YORKSHIRE DALES CYCLE WAY**
- **WEST YORKSHIRE CYCLE WAY**
- **MOUNTAIN BIKING - WEST & SOUTH YORKSHIRE**
- **AIRE VALLEY BIKING GUIDE**
- **CALDERDALE BIKING GUIDE**
- **GLASGOW Clyde Valley & Loch Lomond**

- **WALKING COUNTRY TRIVIA QUIZ**

Over 1000 questions on the great outdoors

Send S.A.E. for a detailed catalogue and pricelist